DIARY OF A CONSPIRACY THEORIST.

SCOTT ANDERSON

Dedication

This book is dedicated to those who stood their ground under immense pressure and held true to themselves.

Without you, we would have lost already.

The content contained within this book may not be reproduced, duplicated or transmitted without direct written permission from the author or the publisher.

Under no circumstances will any blame or legal responsibility be held against the publisher, or author, for any damages, reparation, or monetary loss due to the information contained within this book, either directly or indirectly.

Legal Notice:

This book is copyright protected. It is only for personal use. You cannot amend, distribute, sell, use, quote or paraphrase any part, or the content within this book, without the consent of the author or publisher.

Disclaimer Notice:

Please note the information contained within this document is for educational and entertainment purposes only. All effort has been executed to present accurate, up to date, reliable, complete information. No warranties of any kind are declared or implied. Readers acknowledge that the author is not engaged in the rendering of legal, financial, medical or professional advice. The content within this book has been derived from various sources. Please consult a licensed professional before attempting any techniques outlined in this book.

By reading this document, the reader agrees that under no circumstances is the author responsible for any losses, direct or indirect, that are incurred as a result of the use of the information contained within this document, including, but not limited to, errors, omissions, or inaccuracies.

© Copyright 2023

Contents

Dedication 2
The Beginning 6
Escape from Reality 38
Oblivious.. 51
They are Lying... 78
Opening up... 88
Who, Why, How? 99
Where Next? 118

The Beginning

It was 2019 and I had been quietly working away as a Civil Site Engineer when my mind begun to think about the future and how long it had been since there was a crisis or event that majorly impacted society. In recent years of course we had the destruction of the Twin Towers in America in September 2001 and what seemed to be a perpetual "war on terror" thus culminating in a US led coalition to the invasion Iraq and Afghanistan. It is harder to think of a time where public anxiety was as high as it was then until the events that were to unfold in 2020. Osama Bin Laden, leader of Al-Qaeda was the baddy, and the public anxiety and worry seemed to never really lift until the Barack Obama announced that US special forces had killed him. I'd always found it strange why they boarded his body onto USS Carl Vinson and buried him at sea. This man is supposed to have orchestrated the death of thousands, yet the American government decided they would take into account the political and religious beliefs of this alleged mass-murderer. Not that I am saying Bin Laden is innocent, but not even so much as picture of the most wanted man in the planet? They decided to respect the Islamic way and bury him at sea within twenty-four hours of his death and apparently decided against burying him on land so his grave wouldn't become a shrine to his followers. Yet in the second Gulf war, after capturing Saddam Hussain, you could watch his hanging online and still can today.

In 2003 over a million people protested on the streets of London against the invasion of Iraq, yet it still went ahead. The normal person you meet in the street has no time or place for war but this is a prime example of we heard and listened but do not care and we are doing it anyway. The government does not care about you. Never has, and it never will.

It's little inconsistencies and incidents like this whilst growing up as a young teenager that triggered a refusal to almost take anything governments, particularly the US & UK say, at face value.

It just didn't make sense.

With events like this in mind, I begun to look for alternative views on things.

Are we supposed to just nod and be dragged along for the ride? Every government wants its citizens to back them when they make a decision.

What if they used certain tools at their disposal to make this happen? They told us Saddam Hussain was using Chemical weapons in Iraq. That was a lie. Millions died as a result, including many of our own service men and women.

Remember Colin Powell, Secretary of State held up a tube filled a white powder that was supposed to be Anthrax as he made his case for war in front of the United Nations? This is the deadly Anthrax that can kill through inhalation, by entering through the skin, or intestinally and is fatal in seventy-five percent of cases.

We are supposed to believe this.

It was most likely filled with sugar or salt from Powell's breakfast table that morning, in my opinion.

I will never forget the bombing campaign that ensued, lighting up the Iraqi sky, it looked like they went hell for leather. I can still see the image in my head as I watched the television with my parents.

As John Steinbeck says *"All war is a symptom of man's failure as a thinking animal"*. Or even as Achilles supposedly once said *"Imagine a king who fight's his own battles, wouldn't that be a sight?"*

Wouldn't it just.

Even as a young teenager, certain things just didn't sit right with me. I was always inquisitive and looking for answers. I remember being in secondary school and in a particular class we were asked to take in newspapers to read. I remember reading something about Iran and the level of fear-mongering was off the scale. I thought to myself, why is there so much evil in the world? How can certain individuals and governments regard life so cheaply? You'd literally have to be psychotic to send young men and women to war, knowing many of them may never return. And for what? Oil or Global status?

They can't be human I used to think to myself.

When you see how things aren't quite as portrayed, you begin to ask questions about other things…if we went to the Moon in 1969, why haven't we been back especially with improved technology?

For example, I always find it amusing that we have been using rockets or jet propulsion technology since the 1920's and over 100 years later we are expected to believe

this is the extent of our advancement. There also has to be millions of planets in the universe, yet we are expected to believe we must be the only one of our kind. That seems very closed minded to me.

Even the voting system is laughable. We basically have two main parties, Labour or Conservative, or Republican or Democrat in the US and the other smaller parties don't get a look in. Two cheeks of the same arse. Is it designed to be this way? I'd argue yes. Pretending to be opposition to each party whilst politicians from both sides are balls deep in corruption, ripping off the working man whilst claiming hundreds of thousands of pounds a year in expenses.

A politician is the only job where you get promoted for being inept.

What's that? You made a mess of being Transport Minister, that's okay we'll make you Education Minister this time. Have you ever noticed that certain faces seem to stay in politics for what seems to be forever? The Blair's, the

Bush's the Biden's and Clinton's. They never seem to go away. Balls deep in corruption doesn't go far enough.

Tony Benn a former British politician puts it brilliantly *"In the course of my life I have developed five little democratic questions. If one meets a powerful person--Adolf Hitler, Joe Stalin or Bill Gates--ask them five questions: "What power have you got? Where did you get it from? In whose interests do you exercise it? To whom are you accountable? And how can we get rid of you?" If you cannot get rid of the people who govern you, you do not live in a democratic system."*

As time went on, I looked more into things such as Agenda 21/30 and where certain groups wanted to take the world and society. Why do these powerful groups behind governments want us to live like Orwell's Nineteen eighty-four, where you can't say what you feel or do as you, please and to keep us in our settlement zones? Why were our governments signed up to such agendas like Sustainable Development Goals and the 4th Industrial Revolution? Why were the public not informed of this properly and given the choice to vote? Because if we really knew why they were doing it, they would never have got this far. You could also argue that if voting ever made a difference they would never let you do it. The question is why are

they doing is and how will it be brought in? This led me to people like David Icke and others who were very well researched and could join the dots and put it in an understandable way, especially for a teenager who didn't really comprehend the severity of it all. I think many of us are guilty of knowing what was coming but watching from a distance, waiting for the tsunami of Orwellian dystopic totalitarianism to arrive but not quite knowing how or when it would be implemented by those at the helm.

Weren't we in for a shock huh?

As I mentioned earlier, I was just quietly working away and getting on with life, still reading up on things, still watching from an afar and as we came towards the end of 2019 I had begun to wonder where the next crisis would come from.

Financial crash, I thought. That's how they, the powers at be, the elites, the hidden hand, whatever you want to call them will begin to implement this 10-year plan leading up to 2030. Of course, it doesn't end there, but they have to start it somewhere and I had a feeling the mother of all crashes was coming in 2020. I decided to get Income

Protection Insurance, just in case. It may have been fruitless had something happened but it at least gave me some peace of mind. I felt I needed to warn others and told several members of my family my line of thinking so they could prepare too. I kept phoning my brother and saying

"I'm telling you something is coming; I just know it. There's going to be another financial crash, you need to get this too."

I'd just get his typical blasé response *"aye later, mind me."*

Financial crashes are supposed to happen around every decade and two-thousand and eight was when the last had occurred. It was now nearly two-thousand and twenty, we were overdue and I thought a crash was imminent.

When you also consider that it appeared a cashless society was the plan, with being able to pay with your phone or contactless very much on the rise, and the introduction of crypto currencies it seemed an attempted switch was inevitable.

For me it was just a case of not if, but when.

You don't have to think too hard as to why a cashless society would be catastrophic for democracy and the freedom of the individual:

-No more jobs for cash (homers etc)

-Potential to have money stolen via hacking and cyber crime

-Rural communities may not have as much access due to internet connectivity

-All too easy to spend money as you can't physically see or track what you spend

-No access to bank account due to energy black outs caused by natural disasters or faults

-None of the memories to look forward to that we once had as children, a pound under your pillow after your tooth fell out, money in birthday cards or from grandparents, or some pennies for a sweetie.

And most important of all, the government can say what you spend, how you spend it and when you spend it and also link it to your social credit score. You only have to look at China to see how that works with their social credit system. Criticise the government? You aren't going on that train today. Did something that the authorities perceive as bad, and you aren't doing a thing without the say so of the government. That should act as a warning and should send alarm bells ringing to western citizens. There may be an initial convenience in being cashless, but that's how they will sell the Trojan horse to us, in my opinion.

I'll stick to good old hard cash thanks.

Back at work and still getting the feeling something big was around the corner and having gave myself a bit of peace of mind with the Income Protection Cover, the Christmas holidays had come around and I was quite relaxed knowing I was prepared for what was to come in the New Year.

It'll be alright. I thought, I'm well covered. I've got this.

Boy, how wrong I was.

And We Are Off...

It was now 2020 and I had returned from the Christmas holidays, quite relaxed and not thinking too much about the financial crash I had in my head before the two-week break. It was good to get back to work and get back in the swing of things as you are normally finding your feet again for the first week. The project I had been working on was a new Primary School, nearby a small retail area.

A couple of weeks would go by and then in the media I'd hear whispers of a virus in China. I never really paid any attention to it as you'd occasionally read things in the newspapers about a virus in a foreign country or some Flu that animals may have. They never seemed to amount to much. It soon became clear this was different. Very different.

The way the media had been talking about this virus made me sit up and pay attention. This wasn't the normal illness or Flu that would be read about in a foreign country.

The WHO (World Health Organisation) declared the outbreak a Public Health Emergency of International Concern in January 2020.

Images began to appear showing large excavators shifting ground to leave a platform in which the Chinese claimed they were going to build a 1000 bed hospital in under two weeks. Using 4000 workers they achieved this and the Huoshenshan Hospital opened on February 3rd 2020, having only started the construction phase on January the 24th 2020. Normally as a Civil site engineer, I would have said that such a short timescale would be inconceivable. Although you could argue the relevant standards and checks may not be that of UK standard, it was still some feat. This also added to the intrigue around what was happening.

Why so much panic?

What is this virus?

What is it capable of?

Seeing these images and the video footage of the excavators made me wonder what the hell was going on. It just didn't sit right with me and I continued to watch the news closely and watch the story develop.

The media then began to point the blame at a wet market in Wuhan, where the first cases of the virus, now known as SARS-CoV-2 or Covid-19 were supposed to have originated. A WHO investigation in Wuhan led to the hypothesis that it was transmitted from Bats via another animal to humans. Then as this was reported, then came the typical construction site banter that ensued,

"Ahh! bloody Chinese, they'll eat anything" **and** *"I'll not be having a Chinese this weekend!"*.

Images and videos started to appear in what showed Chinese citizens appearing to drop dead in the middle of the street. Literally just walking along, pausing and then dropping to the ground. It was like something out of a horror movie.

Hmm I thought, this gets weirder by the day.

Cases of this new Coronavirus then continued to spread and appear in countries outside of China. Countries like the United States, Taiwan, Malaysia and Singapore were beginning to find cases. What is a case? I'll talk more on that later. The Chinese authorities decided to lockdown Wuhan, the city of its alleged origin. A city of 11 million people, no travel in or out. Not allowed out of your home unless to it was to collect essential goods such as food etc. As China "locked down" more of its cities, after the World Health Organisation declaring an international emergency, their leader and Director-General Tedros Adhanom Ghebreyesus praised China for its handling of the situation. China was known for being authoritarian, but this was next level. Global cases soon surpassed 100,000 and one of the main countries who appeared to be affected most was Italy, in particular the region of Lombardy, which with a simple Google search at the time showed to be an industrial zone with bad air and it was common for elderly residents to have respiratory illnesses. Was this a contributing factor? It was still just mainly cases; some were dying but it seemed to be thousands of cases.

How ill were they?

What was the symptoms?

Were people dropping dead in the street all round the world?

Eventually the symptoms were disclosed and they were the following:

-Fever or change in temperature

-A continuous cough

-Loss of taste and smell

-Aches and pains

-Sore throat

-Headache

-And Diarrhoea.

This all seemed pretty standard Cold/Flu symptoms to me, how and why are people dropping dead in the street? Note that dropping dead in the street isn't included.

Why is the death toll beginning to ramp up?

It was those inconsistencies again.

The global reaction continued to escalate and other nations were beginning to mention that they may also impose lockdowns like China did.

Back at work and the common theme coming from the guys I worked with was the same.

"I'll just get it and get it over and done with" and

"it'll just be like the Flu; it'll be fine".

That was all very well until our own Prime Minister Boris Johnson begun to flirt with the idea of restrictions and measures.

The mood on site had changed. All of a sudden it was taken seriously and the uncertainty clearly started to fill the air. Nobody knew how this would pan out, as this wasn't your typical pandemic preparedness plan. This was new. A world-wide lockdown had never been done before. I was beginning to think I may have made the right decision getting Income

Protection insurance. If we were locked down, nobody knew how long for and if we would be paid by our employers. The look on the faces around me said it all.

We knew we were next.

On 16th of March 2020, Johnson announced that there would be restrictions in what he called *"the national fightback against the new coronavirus"*.

The body of his speech went as follows:

"Today, we need to go further, because according to SAGE [the Scientific Advisory Group for Emergencies] it looks as though we're now approaching the fast growth part of the upward curve.

And without drastic action, cases could double every 5 or 6 days.

So, first, we need to ask you to ensure that if you or anyone in your household has one of those two symptoms, then you should stay at home for fourteen days.

That means that, if possible, you should not go out even to buy food or essentials, other than for exercise, and in that case at a safe distance from others. If necessary, you should ask for help from others for your daily necessities. And if that is not possible, then you should do what you can to limit your social contact when you leave the house to get supplies.

And even if you don't have symptoms and if no one in your household has symptoms, there is more that we need you to do now.

So, second, now is the time for everyone to stop non-essential contact with others and to stop all unnecessary travel.

We need people to start working from home where they possibly can. And you should avoid pubs, clubs, theatres and other such social venues."

These are not the words you'd expect to hear from your Prime Minister as he addressed the nation. It just didn't seem real, yet it was happening so fast. It was hard to comprehend, but you didn't really have time to think about it as the whole scale of the situation just seemed to explode at an exponential rate.

Rumours started to circulate and the writing was on the wall and it was only a matter of time. It was going to be a week at most before the whole of the United Kingdom would be in full lockdown, you could sense it.

This sent people absolutely crazy and they ended up panic buying from supermarkets. People were buying things like pasta, tinned vegetables, medication and hand gel. The item that appeared to be most treasured by the public though was toilet roll. It got so bad that supermarkets had to ration how many items you could buy per person. I remember it clear as day, being on the phone to my Mum and we were discussing the fact it looked like were about to go in to a hard lockdown with more severe restrictions and I remember sitting in this retail park car park which was just outside the construction site and looking across at the shops.

Cars were whizzing about everywhere, and you could see everyone had the same thoughts. You were forced into panic buying even if you didn't want to because if you didn't there would be nothing left.

I remember going to get some shopping in Lidl's as it may be my last chance before the lockdown would start and I had never seen it so busy. Not even at Christmas time. The queue was reaching the back walls of the store. It was absolutely crazy and the shelves were absolutely empty. It reminded me of a scene from the film World War Z. There were even videos online of people fighting over toilet roll. People were getting arrested over toilet roll, yes! Toilet roll! Toilet roll! No wonder those cute little Andrex puppies in the adverts look so happy, their owners must have been laughing all the way to the bank! At the time of all of this happening, there were only around 300 Covid-19 cases in the UK, 300 out of a population of around 67 million people. It was still early days but thinking of it rationally and logically, it was a Coronavirus, not the Black Plague.

It wasn't going to wipe everybody out. Surely it made sense to shield the vulnerable and let the young and fit carry on and keep the economy ticking over? Hand sanitiser was the other prize item. People had realised they could take advantage of the panic and they were being sold online for all sorts of prices. There were even stories of distilleries making hand sanitiser.

Before we knew it, Boris Johnson was addressing the nation again. This time though, we knew what was coming. Boris with his just-out-of-bed hair, scruffy look and waffling tone of voice, I'd always felt like nobody really paid too much attention to him. This was different. You couldn't just ignore what he was saying as everything around you, everything you knew, that you were familiar with, was going to become completely unrecognisable. Before he had even started speaking the texts on my phone were coming in thick and fast about whether today was going to be the day the lockdown was announced.

The crux of his speech went like this:

"Because the critical thing we must do is stop the disease spreading between households.

That is why people will only be allowed to leave their home for the following very limited purposes:

shopping for basic necessities, as infrequently as possible

one form of exercise a day – for example a run, walk, or cycle – alone or with members of your household;

any medical need, to provide care or to help a vulnerable person; and

travelling to and from work, but only where this is absolutely necessary and cannot be done from home.

That's all – these are the only reasons you should leave your home.

You should not be meeting friends. If your friends ask you to meet, you should say No.

You should not be meeting family members who do not live in your home.

You should not be going shopping except for essentials like food and medicine – and you should do this as little as you can. And use food delivery services where you can.

If you don't follow the rules the police will have the powers to enforce them, including through fines and dispersing gatherings.

To ensure compliance with the Government's instruction to stay at home, we will immediately:

close all shops selling non-essential goods, including clothing and electronic stores and other premises including libraries, playgrounds and outdoor gyms, and places of worship;

we will stop all gatherings of more than two people in public – excluding people you live with;

and we'll stop all social events, including weddings, baptisms and other ceremonies, but excluding funerals.

Parks will remain open for exercise but gatherings will be dispersed.

No Prime Minister wants to enact measures like this.

I know the damage that this disruption is doing and will do to people's lives, to their businesses and to their jobs.

And that's why we have produced a huge and unprecedented programme of support both for workers and for business.

And I can assure you that we will keep these restrictions under constant review. We will look again in three weeks, and relax them if the evidence shows we are able to.

But at present there are just no easy options. The way ahead is hard, and it is still true that many lives will sadly be lost.

And yet it is also true that there is a clear way through.

Day by day we are strengthening our amazing NHS with 7500 former clinicians now coming back to the service.

With the time you buy – by simply staying at home – we are increasing our stocks of equipment.

We are accelerating our search for treatment.

We are pioneering work on a vaccine.

And we are buying millions of testing kits that will enable us to turn the tide on this invisible killer.

I want to thank everyone who is working flat out to beat the virus.

Everyone from the supermarket staff to the transport workers to the carers to the nurses and doctors on the frontline.

But in this fight, we can be in no doubt that each and every one of us is directly enlisted.

Each and every one of us is now obliged to join together.

To halt the spread of this disease.

To protect our NHS and to save many more thousands of lives."

It's a long speech to include but I felt it will turn out to be a historic point in history and important to emphasize the scale of what was actually happening. Hopefully the last of its kind we'll ever hear.

I feel in years to come, should I ever end up with Grandchildren and were to tell them what happened, I would want them to see, understand and recognise what happened to ensure they would never let it happen to them which is partly why I decided to write this book

Going back to Johnson's speech.

Basically, your life was turned upside down and you couldn't do the normal day to day things that you would normally.

The message was soon repeated everywhere. Protect the NHS and rather sickeningly they urged people not to kill Granny. This was clearly a psychological operation, an operation where you were the enemy. It was the biggest PSYOP in history and the government was waging a war against its own people in a quest for compliance. Comply and you will get your freedom back, or so people were led to believe, which was just ridiculous. They kept moving the goal posts all the time, extending the lockdown anytime there were more cases which was just ridiculous. The vaccine was the ticket out of this they would say. I didn't want a vaccine, I just wanted to go to work and live life and if I got this "virus" then it was on me. If you were afraid of catching it, then you should stay at home which would make sense but they had an answer for that, asymptomatic transmission. Eh? I thought. Pre 2020, if I had the cold or flu, I wouldn't go see my grandparents which I think is how most people behaved. Which is common sense. The government were saying that you cannot see them as you may pass it on without knowing you even have it. What complete bollocks. It's how this whole scam was kept going. Asymptomatic transmission was the glue that held the pieces together and without it the whole thing would crumble. What a genius idea, let people think they might have a deadly virus without knowing they have it and bombarding their frightened minds with constant propaganda and fear mongering creating the desired compliance. You have got to hand it to them. It was perfect.

Going out for the first time whilst under house arrest and getting my daily exercise for that day, it was something like I never thought I'd experience. It reminded me of the film I Am Legend, or 28 Days Later when the main character Jim wakes from his coma to find the hospital uninhabited and walks the streets to find them empty, lifeless and eerily quiet. Just open spaces of nothingness. There wasn't a soul anywhere to be seen or heard, the roads were empty, everything was closed and the constant barrage of fear had clearly done its job. The world has literally stopped. I was going out several times a day for long walks and on most occasions, I was clocking 20,000 steps on my Garmin watch, if there was anything that would keep me sane in these mad times it was exercise and fresh air.

Out on my long walks I begun to think more about things and think about what was happening and why, and it soon became very clear early on. It was such things like Google's Deepmind (a subsidiary of Google) was invited to the SAGE (Scientific Advisory Group for Emergencies) professionals who would not be initially named. Why's that might you ask?

It could be that some of them were psychologists such a Susan Michie who is a member of the Communist Party.

Nothing to worry about, I'm sure.

SAGE was also supported by SPI-B (Independent Scientific Pandemic Insights Group on Behaviours) who say on the Government website

"SPI-B provides behavioural science advice aimed at anticipating and helping people adhere to interventions that are recommended by medical or epidemiological experts."

What they really mean is they use psychological and behavioural techniques to ensure compliance to aid those creating the policies or in other words to get you to do as your told.

Below is just an example of the techniques they would use which became a major part of their propaganda and you can clearly see the part on the left-hand side where it says "Use media to increase perceived level of threat." And "Use of media to increase sense of responsibility to others"

Don't kill Granny remember? Save the NHS?

Appendix B: APEASE evaluation grid for options to rapidly increase general social distancing

Option	Evaluation criteria (APEASE)					
	Acceptability	Practicability	Effectiveness	Affordability	Spill-over effects	Equity
1. Provide clear, precise, credible guidance about specific behaviours	HIGH	HIGH	HIGH IF ACCOMPANIED BY OTHER OPTIONS	HIGH	POSITIVE	UNCERTAIN
2. Use media to increase sense of personal threat	HIGH	HIGH	HIGH IF ACCOMPANIED BY OTHER OPTIONS	HIGH	COULD BE NEGATIVE	UNCERTAIN
3. Use media to increase sense of responsibility to others	HIGH	HIGH	HIGH IF ACCOMPANIED BY OTHER OPTIONS	HIGH	POSITIVE	UNCERTAIN
4. Use media to promote positive messaging around actions	HIGH	HIGH	HIGH IF ACCOMPANIED BY OTHER OPTIONS	HIGH	POSITIVE	UNCERTAIN
5. Tailor messaging	HIGH	HIGH	HIGH IF ACCOMPANIED BY OTHER OPTIONS	HIGH	UNCERTAIN	UNCERTAIN
6. Use and promote social approval for desired behaviours	HIGH	HIGH	COULD BE HIGH	HIGH	POSITIVE	UNCERTAIN
7. Consider enacting legislation to compel required behaviours	COULD BE HIGH IF EQUITY ISSUES ADDRESSED	DEPENDS ON TIMESCALE	COULD BE HIGH IF ACCEPTABLE AND ENFORCED	UNCERTAIN DEPENDING ON LEVEL OF ENFORCMENT	COULD BE NEGATIVE	COULD BE NEGATIVE
8. Consider use of social disapproval for failure to comply	UNCERTAIN	HIGH	COULD BE HIGH IF ACCOMPANIED BY OTHER MEASURES	HIGH	COULD BE NEGATIVE	COULD BE NEGATIVE
9. Develop and mobilise adequately resources community infrastructure	HIGH	VARIABLE	HIGH	MODERATE	POSITIVE	POSITIVE
10. Provide financial and material resources to mitigate effects of measures on equity	HIGH	VARIABLE	HIGH	UNCERTAIN	POSITIVE	POSITIVE

Stay home and stay safe?

"Use and promote social approval for desired behaviours" is another, as we know people like to virtue signal and show what a good citizen they were by following the rules, thus keeping people in line by fear of being publicly outed.

Facebook was the main platform in which neighbours in the street would call out their other neighbours who broke the rules.

The Karen's and Kevin's as they are known wouldn't take long to let the world know their disgust at seeing Joe Bloggs go out twice that day and how irresponsible he was and that his actions could result in somebodies' death, and of course the obligatory **"Stay safe and stay home!"** at the bottom of the post. It was useful idiots like this who kept others in line, pressuring people and with the help of the media portraying that this was the general consensus of the population further increasing the social pressure to comply where most people probably really didn't care, were enjoying furlough (the scheme set up by the government to ensure you got paid) and were willing to take the experimental jab to get on with their lives. Crazy, but people will almost do anything it would appear to keep their materialistic and consumer lifestyles going.

Who needs enemies with neighbours like that?

Furlough was another tool to keep the population sweet, just like asymptomatic transmission, without it there would have been no "pandemic" and without people being paid to sit at home, there would have been an eruption of protests.

Can you imagine if the government told people to stay at home with no pay?

It would have never got off the ground, people were pacified by the government printing money for fun, yet very few considered the consequences of such a move. People were happy to sit at home, the weather was the best it had been in years (almost conveniently) the salaries and wages were still coming in, and the Tik Tok videos were being made, Amazon was delivering anything you needed at the click of a button. Some just had it too good. Not everyone had it this way of course, people that live in apartment buildings or blocks of flats with no gardens, some with kids. They must have found it excruciating. Some were also alone, with family members most likely not wanting to see them for fear of getting the virus. I can only imagine it must have been horrendous.

Even if you did believe the lies or get sucked in by the propaganda aided by the behavioural psychologists at SPI-B, if you lived alone and your friends and family abided by the rules set, it was going to get lonely. We may have modern technology and apps like Zoom, WhatsApp, Facetime etc. but you can't beat proper social interaction. The isolation was going to affect people big time.

Escape from Reality

Is its little wonder that mental health problems are going through the roof and more and more are turning to alcohol, most likely for some escapism?

According to the ONS (Office for National Statistics):

- In 2021, there were 9,641 deaths (14.8 per 100,000 people) from alcohol-specific causes registered in the UK, the highest number on record.

- The number recorded in 2021 was 7.4% higher than in 2020 (8,974 deaths; 14.0 per 100,000) and 27.4% higher than in 2019 (7,565 deaths; 11.8 per 100,000), the last pre-coronavirus (COVID-19) pandemic year.

I won't lie, I ended up getting very depressed during the lockdown as I didn't know what the future held, I didn't know if I'd return to a job, I had none of my normal routine which I didn't appreciate previously how it positively affected my wellbeing. I felt I was on a different planet as it appeared most were buying the "pandemic" and you couldn't have a conversation with anyone without either holding your tongue or telling them it was a load of nonsense and most likely falling out. I ended up drinking too much myself once I'd injured my knee running and then the daily routine of exercise stopped, it was then the go to for my own escapism from the ever-increasing madness in the world. Only now three years later am I back in the gym and replacing bad habits with good ones. I was one of the lucky ones though, my immediate family were all mostly onside and shared the same opinion that this whole thing was a scam. It was only my father's side of my family that stopped speaking to me and my siblings due to our "conspiracy theories" or opinions.

I often wonder what is worse, me not speaking or reaching out knowing it there is no deadly pandemic or them not reaching out thinking there is one?

I know of situations where people have lost all contact with their children or parents or other family members, and the worst thing about all this is they were taken in by a psychological operation carried out by those who are supposed to serve us. It's disgusting and we must never forgive the perpetrators for what they have done.

No doubt people will have stayed inside apart from there one chance of exercise a day looking at the almost foreign sunshine through their windows. I cannot remember the last time we had weather like that, I'd have to go back to me being around 7 or 8 years old. The only good thing I can say about the lockdowns apart from the weather, was it put a lot of things in perspective like family with whom I spent a lot of time with and almost daily I'd visit my parents during the lockdown. It made me realise that material possessions don't really matter; they come and go. There was more to life and I decided that once this was over, if it ever was going to be over that I'd spend more time doing things that made me happy than being on the constant search for something more.

I know there were some who questioned the gyms being closed as if this was about health surely, you'd have wanted healthy people to at least maintain good health in a situation where if you had a low or compromised immune system you may have been more at risk to the alleged virus.

The gym or exercise often acts as someone's therapy and they use the endorphins released after such an activity to maintain a positive mental well-being. In short, it would have no doubt kept many sane and in a better psychological state.

I previously mentioned how exercise kept me sane and in a good state of mind and when that stopped and bad habits crept in, the reason to get up in the morning was becoming less and less important. I ended up gaining four stone in total between the lockdown starting and by the time they had stopped completely. I just totally lost all motivation, discipline and desire to do anything. I was totally depressed. I had little or no interest in anything, I wasn't interested in music which I love, I didn't care what was happening with my football team, I just didn't really see the point. It was hard to not feel like we were onto a loser and that we just might not come out the other side of this and stop the whole agenda from being carried out, or the Great Reset as it was beginning to be known as. The fact is whether you believed the narrative or not it was still a toll mentally.

People were scared senseless and that constant fear of being infected at any moment couldn't have done any good at all. It was also a struggle for those who knew it was bullshit as I'd come to realise as the protests begun to happen and I'd also make a case for saying more so than the frightened public that thought their government had their best interests at heart.

I remember getting a message from someone who I won't name basically calling for help. Absolutely desperate for some normal social interaction. Myself and another member of my family went around to their house and they said they had been watching Nicola Sturgeon's daily briefings, had been listening and following everything she had been saying and that none of her family wanted to see her and she just couldn't take it anymore. This was clear as she was visibly shaking.

It reminded me of how sick these bastards are and what they were doing to people who really just wanted to get on with their life and be left alone. It makes my blood boil.

According to the website Cygnet Health:

New figures from Cygnet Health Care reveal the impact Covid-19 and lockdown had on children's mental health with a leading psychiatrist saying more young people are

seeking help with issues such as anxiety, depression and disordered eating.

Referrals to Cygnet's psychiatric intensive care units in its Child and Adolescent Mental Health (CAMHS) hospitals more than doubled between 2019 and 2022.

Prior to the global virus in 2019, 255 referrals of young people were made to psychiatric intensive care units run by Cygnet Health Care. By 2022, this had risen to 596, an increase of 134%.

Admissions to the units saw a 41% increase in that time.

There an increase in the number of young people presenting with issues such as low mood, insomnia, stress, anxiety, anger, irritability, emotional exhaustion, depression and post-traumatic stress symptoms following lockdown.

One of the biggest increases in presentation was seen in disordered eating.

Similarly, referrals to its inpatient acute services rose by 61%, increasing from 668 young people in 2019, to 1078 throughout 2022.

Dr Triveni Joshi, who is a consultant psychiatrist and also Medical Director at Cygnet Hospital Joyce Parker, which offers hospital admissions for young people dealing with mental health difficulties says

"Lockdowns would have played a massive part in the decline in mental health for young people and is a leading cause in the spike in numbers of young people needing support.

She said: *"We won't know for many years whether the virus itself disturbed young people's neurological development but we have emerging evidence which tells us about the detrimental impact of lockdown," she explained.*

"It impacted young people's mental health and wellbeing severely, particularly those who had pre-existing mental health conditions.

In my view the biggest concern was the isolation. We know that lack of socialisation is a key factor in depression. The young people became trapped in their homes.

"They were missing social contact and no way of engaging in activities which would have previously

boosted their mental health such as sports clubs and activities with their friends.

Not having that outlet, as well as the huge sense of anxiety about what was happening to the world around them, would have been overwhelming and little wonder they struggled."

Whilst I don't agree that the virus had disturbed people neurological development, I'd argue that constantly living in fear of it will have. Particularly those of a young age that may be in Primary School, missing out on a tonne of social development and learning.

Children watch and observe adults as they develop and all they saw was fear and panic and they will have picked up on that.

According to the Spectator, there are "Ghost children". These are school pupils who never returned after the lockdown and some of the statistics are cause for concern:

"In the last full school term – the autumn of 2019, shortly before the start of the pandemic – just 60,202 pupils were defined as 'severely absent': that is, spending more time out of classrooms than in them. Since then, and despite schools opening, this number has shot up. Now 140,000 children are classed as 'severely absent', according to the analysis of official figures by the CSJ – a rise of 134 per cent, or the equivalent of around 140 schools. Despite recent efforts their numbers have continued to surge. Children are turning their backs on education 'at an alarming pace', warns the CSJ."

Is it the anxiety that has been instilled in them by the mainstream media?

Was it the social isolation?

Could it be that they don't want to wear masks and socially distance?

I feel like we will be picking up the pieces for years as we can only guess how being in a lockdown will have affected these kids in the long run.

Another section of the article said:

"Lockdowns proved a disaster for young people at every stage of their development. With all the attention on the elderly, the young were left to cope on their own. It was assumed they'd be resilient. Far from it.

As one primary school teacher said to me: 'It breaks my heart looking at the kids in my class. Either they are crippled with anxiety or jumping off the walls. Basically, they are just not happy."

The journalist speaks of the elderly who were given all the attention which they may have been but that doesn't mean it was the correct attention.

If you call elderly people in care homes who most likely lost hope and passed away not seeing their loved ones on their last days as "attention" then I must be missing something here. Sometimes a visit from family is the only thing that keeps them going.

Take that away and what have you got?

A nurse or carer, masked up telling you that you can't see your family or go outside and it'll all be over once you get your jab, is no way to spend your last days on this earth in my eyes.

What's worse is when they did see family it was through window or as Philip Schofield and Holly Willoughby demonstrated on the TV programme, This Morning, hugging through a sheet of plastic.

Holly and Phil bless them, they must think we are stupid pretending to hug for the first time in months whilst they kept "social distancing" on screen were most likely laughing and joking about it backstage.

What a piss takes.

Some tried to get into care homes to see their loved ones but were denied access although there were stories of some managing to get in and escape with their parent and take them home.

Can you imagine if you knew one of your parents potentially didn't have long left and someone was saying you couldn't see them because you may have a deadly virus which is potentially symptomless?

I know what I'd have said and it's not for writing in this book!

I never really saw the point in some elderly getting the jab either.

Put aside what I really think for a moment and consider whether you vaccinate your elderly relative (some were over 90 years old) and giving them an experimental vaccine for a virus with a 99.7% survival rate? Would it not be better to just feed them properly, look after them well, and provide them with plenty of family love?

Just my opinion of course.

Even if you believe the virus was similar to the flu, which according to the statistics it basically was, was it worth getting ill after the vaccine which many do for a few days after the flu vaccine, which has always made me wonder why people even get it?

It's another Big Pharma scam. They don't even know what strain is going about half the time so how can they give you a vaccine to protect against it? They can't!

When you sit back and take a look at things objectively, there is a lot that goes on in the world that is total B.S and if only some would give it a few seconds though before participating in such absolute nonsense.

Oblivious…

As people grew a little more confidence and started to venture out for their exercise it was the first time, you'd see people not in an online capacity.

It was now you'd actually see how people were thinking and acting.

I used to walk from Inverness to Dochgarroch which is around 3.5 miles there and the same back so it was quite a decent stretch.

On one occasion I remember bumping into a guy I knew who was walking his dog who I'll call Fred. Fred had a degree in economics and was a secondary school teacher and a B & B owner so he wasn't daft or at least I thought he wasn't. We had a bit of chat and the usual how's things. I then asked him what he thought of the whole situation and he said "I think it's great, I'm getting money for the B & B, I'm getting this and that". He rattled off how much money he was getting and I can't remember the figures but put it this way, no wonder he thought it was great.

We both kind of agreed that the virus isn't as bad as they make out, but this is what you were up against.

People were quite happy to take the money, Netflix and chill as they say these days.

Here was a guy with a degree in Economics and he couldn't see the wood for the trees. He was totally oblivious to the fact that the money tree will keep printing and we will be paying for it in big style when it's over.

I appreciate the Furlough scheme might have kept people above water, but the point is we should have never locked down in the first place and told them where to go.

Without such dangling carrots there would have been so much more fury at this one size fits all restrictions.

He was lucky though, there were many who's businesses are no longer open post pandemic and no doubt there are some who lost absolutely everything.

I know the hospitality industry suffered greatly, even after everything opening up again, the confidence wasn't in people to go out and have a good time like before.

People had also gotten used to having a drink in the house. On another occasion on one of my long walks I remember a guy cycling past me on a bike and he said "how's it going Scotty boy?".

I still have no clue who that was to this day.

He had his face covered with a mask, sun glasses on and a hat yet the temperature was in the mid-twenties and he was on his bike, alone.

I also used to frequent the Ness Islands in Inverness a lot, I remember being about to walk over one of the bridges and normally there is plenty room for someone to pass coming in the opposite direction but this young guy with purple and green hair started bawling at me "Get back! Get back! Read the sign, only one person across the bridge at any one time!".

I won't tell you what I said but it starts with F and ends with off.

I clearly must have mistaken his pronouns or something.

Jokes aside, this is what the constant fear mongering stories and daily death count were doing to people.

When have you ever heard the head of a country give a daily death count for any other virus? Never!

In 1968, the Hong Kong Flu was estimated to have killed up to 4 million people worldwide and totalling around 80,000 deaths in the UK, why no lockdowns then? No restrictions or stay at home orders.

Because there is an agenda this time in my opinion which I'll get into shortly.

The most annoying this is people born around this time seem to have totally forgotten about this, probably because they didn't have sign everywhere telling them where to walk, or had to socially distance, wear a mask or be pressured into taking a damn vaccine.

Social media wasn't even around then to discuss online what was going on and to talk about what may or may not be happening.

The powers at be behind this scam could have attempted this power grab then, but in my opinion, they weren't ready, much like the attempt in 2008 with Swine Flu but that attempt was taken apart by whistle-blowers.

I didn't think they had everything in place like they do now and they didn't have the technology.

Smart phones are the gate way and the key to the elite's global system of control.

Tik Tok an app I just cannot stand, it just epitomises modern day society for me.

It's an app where it's users can post videos which is fine, but go have a watch and see for yourself. The most pointless and stupid videos are posted and it just makes you wonder if we actually have any intellect left in western civilisation. What happened to just living in the moment? Without being constantly being stuck to our phone screens all day. The internet and smart phones are the best AND worst inventions at exactly the same time. It's a catch 22 situation.

We can access information that we never could have before at the very touch of a button, but we have also become consumed and engulfed by it, so much so that we

allow it to affect our relationships, mental health and effective use of our time.

Chinese owned international version TikTok, has a Chinese counterpart called Douyin, but the difference in content is night and day. Douyin has more educational content and only allows Chinese content unlike the international version.

Where am I going with this?

Doctors and nurses were obviously still working during the lockdown and according to the government and mainstream media it was our job to protect the NHS.

Within a few weeks it became obvious just how busy nurses had been, totally rushed off their feet....

Not quite how you'd imagine.

I never knew nurses had such talent, were so light on their

feet and could choreograph a routine so good, Strictly, Come Dancing will have participants for years if they were to look to the NHS!

Dancing videos and lots of them and not just in the UK, they were in the USA too. These nurses had so much time on their hands that they could choreograph full dancing routines and they had no issue with rubbing it in our faces. There smiles gleefully lit up the screen as they did their elaborate twists and turns and they didn't care who knew it.

Did it ever occur to any of their brains that, wait, hold on a second, maybe we shouldn't be doing this?

Maybe it isn't right?

Maybe someone will see us?

Will they see my face?

They will find out we aren't busy?

Meanwhile we were trapped in our homes for practically 23 hours a day under the premise of protecting their place of work and to stop it being overwhelmed.

Many treatments cancelled or delayed, diagnoses missed, people dying alone and this is what they were up to.

I'm biting my tongue here.

All this talk of the NHS lacking beds and staff and this is the piss take the public were subjected to, yet very few seemed to grasp that, you know, it may just all be a load of bollocks.

Speaking of NHS beds, see this excerpt from the website The King's Fund:

"NHS hospital beds in England

This briefing uses 1987/88 as the starting point for its analysis – the earliest point from which national data is routinely available. However, the number of NHS beds had been falling for

sometime before this. In 1974 the health service maintained almost 400,000 beds; by 1979/80 the number had dropped to around 350,000.

Between 1987/88 and 2019/20, the total number of NHS hospital beds fell by 53 per cent – from 299,400 to 141,000"

Figure 2 There are around half the number of hospital beds in the English NHS compared to 30 years ago

Number of beds

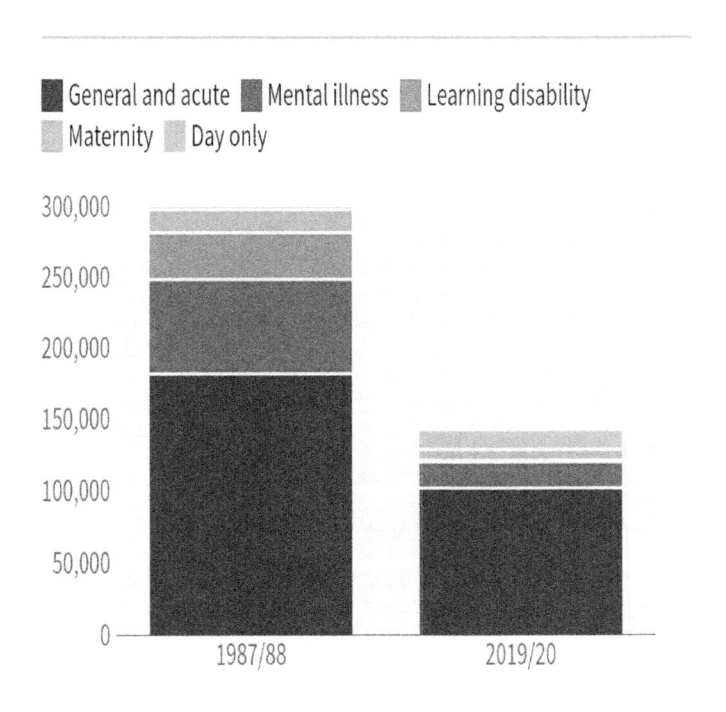

■ General and acute ■ Mental illness ■ Learning disability
■ Maternity ■ Day only

Source: NHS England
From 1987/88 to 2009/10 data were based on an annual snapshot. From 2010/11 the data collection changed and figures are not directly comparable over this period. 2019/20 based on the average of quarterly data over the year. Data not compared to most recent year (2020/21) due to the impact of covid on bed numbers.

The King's Fund〉

chart showing the population of the UK

The UK population was 57million in 1987, and in 2020 it chart has risen to 67 million and counting. The pandemic no longer matters until they then decide it does again as they allow thousands of immigrants to flood the country, staying hotels that have been struggling throughout the last couple of years and now all of a sudden, they are full and guaranteed a good income for the foreseeable future.

The problem is clear to see and doesn't take a brain surgeon (pardon the pun) to figure out why things are the way they stand as this book is being written.

The population has gone up by over 10 million and the number of beds has halved.

For some reason politicians fail to mention this and you have to wonder if this is being done on purpose to bring the National Health Service to its knees and then privatising it, then we will all be paying for our treatment directly.

In my opinion the NHS is purposely being destroyed.

The only is the journalist and broadcaster I have heard actually mention these facts is Richie Allen of his radio show.

Remember those Nightingale hospitals that they spent millions on?

Guess what?

They were never even used.

If they want to save money, why not get rid of the absolutely ridiculous diversity managers and other posts someone with too much time on their hands decided to make up.

The public though were in denial. They refused to see that their demi-gods were not busy and saving lives like they claimed to be doing.

It gets worse, much worse. If ignoring these videos infecting social media globally like a virus were not bad enough, the hand claps into thin air at 8pm every Thursday were.

No, I'm not joking it actually happened.

People would go out into their gardens at 8 o'clock every Thursday and clap into thin air to show their appreciation for the NHS. Pots and pans were brought into the mix and you couldn't ignore it if you tried.

I'd be sitting in my garden or in the house and I'd hear this noise and I'm thinking I didn't know whether to laugh or cry.

The psychological operation, the guilt tripping, the social experiment had worked wonders and you only had to look out your window to see who the biggest virtue signaller was.

This may seem harsh as people were clearly sucked in, but clapping into thin air? Really?

I can't let that one goes without a wee prod.

Intelligence has left the building.

Eventually this all simmered down and the need to show who had the biggest false virtue began to dissipate.

I would remember sitting in my parent's garden and you'd hear it get quieter and quieter as the weeks went on.

If you looked out the window, you'd see your neighbours smiling away, hands in the air and giving it everything they had as they'd turn and give a friendly nod to those who had made the effort on the left and then the same again on the right.

I had to laugh.

Instead of "your Da sells Avon" the playground insult should be "Your Da clapped into thin air".

Then there were also the Black Lives Matter protests where thousands of black people hit the streets to protest against the death of George Floyd at the hands of Police in America. Yet interestingly there appeared to be no spike in virus cases and no condemnation from the authorities, yet any protests against the restrictions was shut down or vilified.

Not that I cared that they were protesting, it just highlights the hypocrisy.

One night myself and my brother attempted to put a banner up on the Ness Bridge which is more or less in the centre of the city.

Before we had even got a chance to tie it up, the Police were upon us like a rash.

Of course, we legged it, we didn't fancy paying the fine.

It was absolutely mental, police both sides of the bridge, they were determined to get us. We ran down to Friars Bridge, where we ran up the steps and just as we got to the top a Police van had just passed and we crossed the road behind it.

Talk about good timing.

We walked through the area of Merkinch and eventually made our way to the canal where they were still chasing us.

I thought to myself "fuck me, think we'd robbed a bank!".

We must have run about 3 or 4 miles that night.

In hindsight we should have just spoke to them, but people weren't acting like they normally do and we didn't know

most of the fines for breaching lockdown rules would eventually be overturned.

It was a good laugh anyway to be fair.

It was crazy times though.

In some countries they even had Police drones with messages from the Police telling them to get home or socially distance. In Singapore, they actually had robotic dogs to ensure you kept your distance. Sci-fi stuff!

People were getting arrested for sitting on park benches alone. Alone!

There were also occasions where my brother who lived in a small village called Dulnain Bridge was getting the Police called on him for taking the kids out of the house and playing on the grass.

What harm they could possibly be doing I do not know; however, I have felt that those who didn't have the choana's to break the rules themselves had to try ruin it for others.

The photo with the *How to Lie with Statistics* book on his left.

Note the mask, either a clear sign they don't work or this is bullshit?

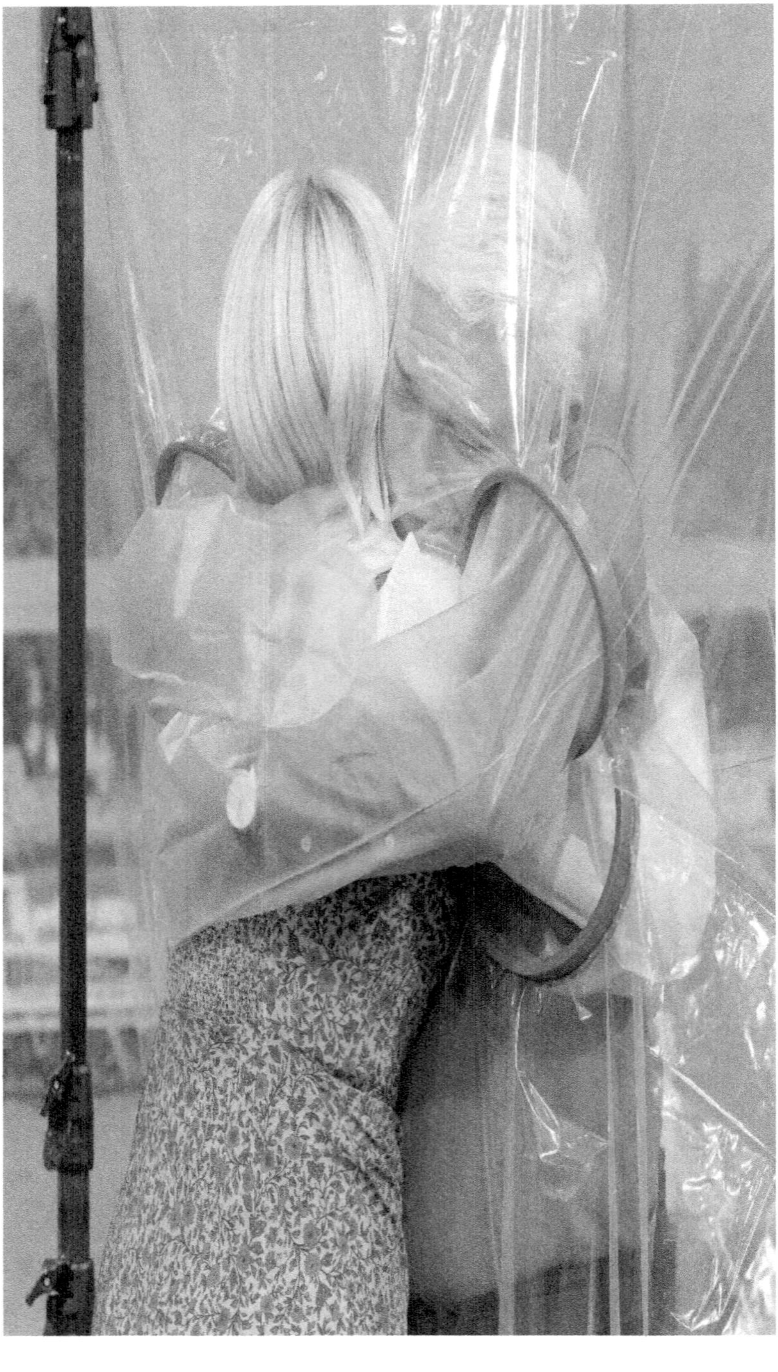

Morning.

"Your Da clapped into thin air"

Boris Johnson addressing the nation.

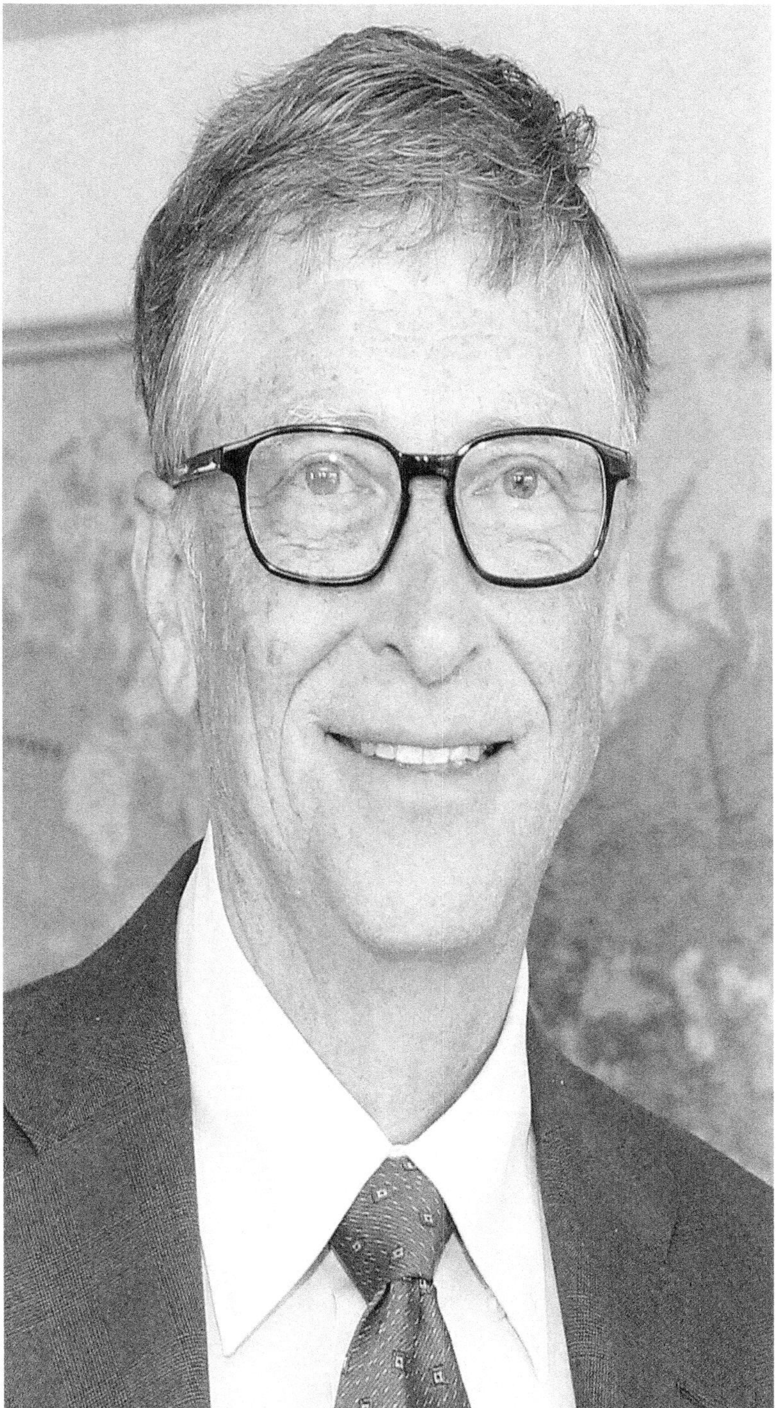

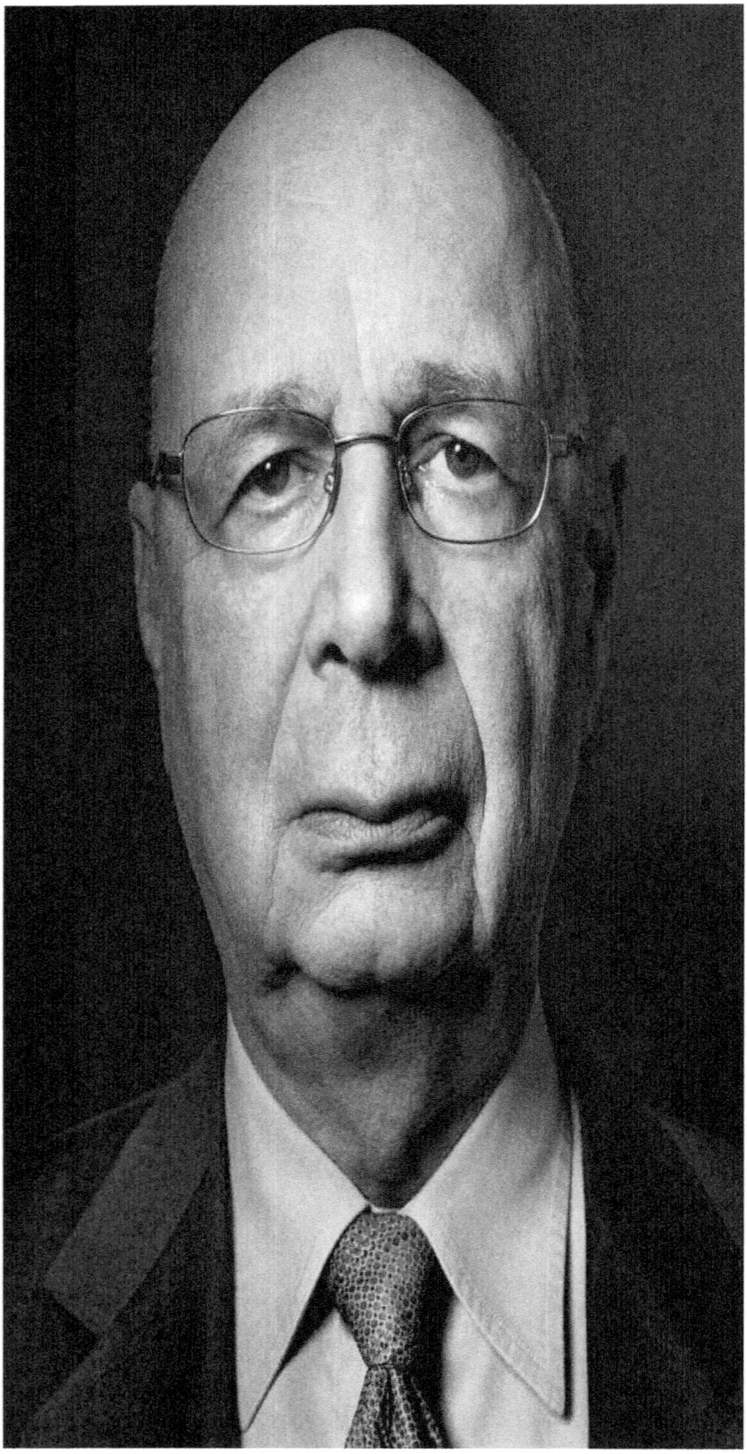

Bill Gates, who famously said in interview that was getting a 20-1 return on vaccines.

Life through a window, the life of a nursing home resident throughout the lockdowns.

Never has the world been so still.

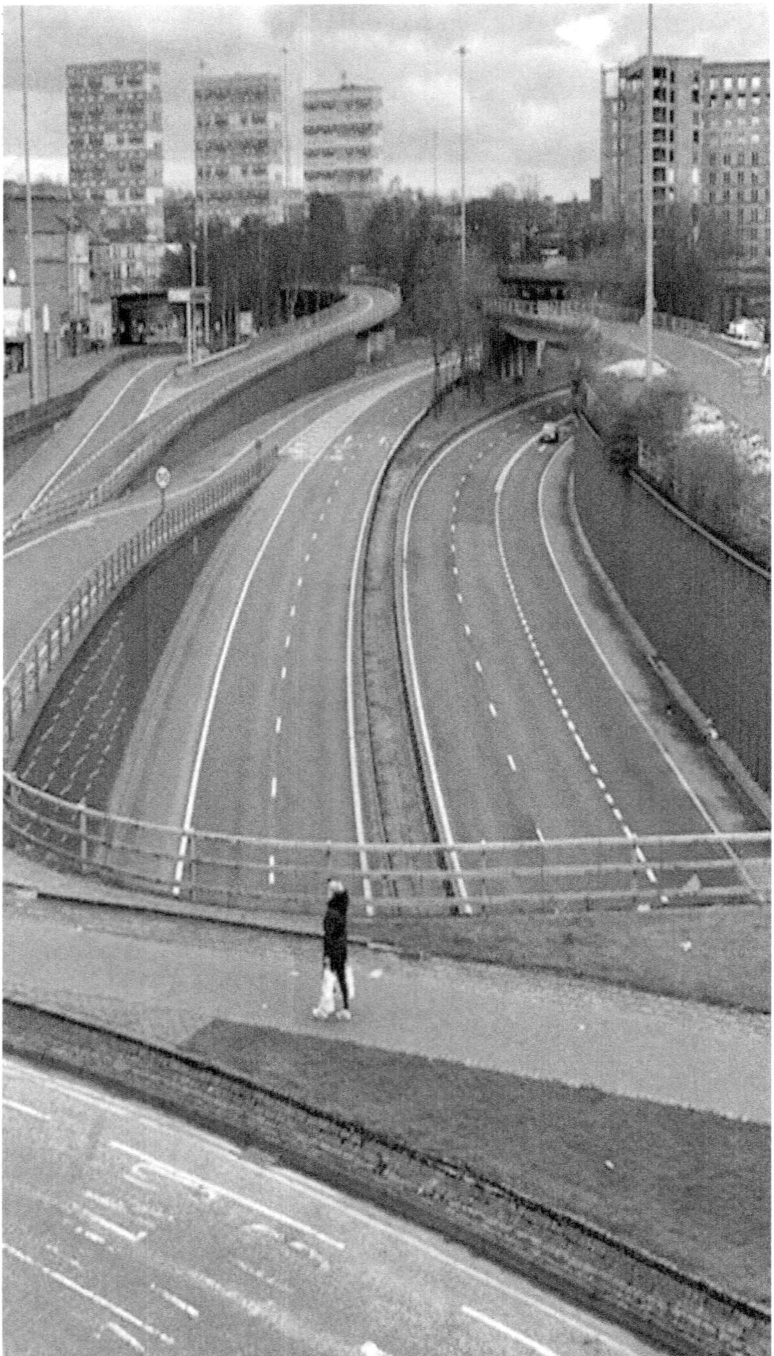

They are Lying…

As time went on it was long before those inconsistencies, I mentioned began to surface which inevitably there always are, simply because they are lying.

If the government and its politicians' lips are moving, it's most likely a lie and most of the time they do not care a jot that you know they are.

I'm sorry to disappoint you if you thought they had your best interest at heart but they clearly do not.

On the 19th of March 2020 Covid-19 was declared by the British government to be a no longer high consequence disease on its website:

"Status of COVID-19

As of 19 March 2020, COVID-19 is no longer considered to be an HCID in the UK. There are many diseases which can cause serious illness which are not classified as HCIDs

"

We were in full lockdown just days later.

Very early on the Chief Medical Officer, Chris Whitty opened his big mouth before getting the memo. At one of the early press conferences his exact words were

"At an individual level the chances of dying from Coronavirus are low.

- Over the whole epidemic, even if there is no vaccine, a high proportion will not get it.
- Of those who do, a significant proportion (exact number not yet clear) have no symptoms
- Of the symptomatic cases, the great majority (around 80%) a mild-moderate disease.

A minority will have to go to hospital, most need only oxygen. The great majority of these will survive.

- A minority of those need ventilation.
- A minority from every age group sadly die with current treatment, but even the oldest group most do not.

He has said this on multiple occasions, reiterating the fact that it is a relatively mild disease, much like the Flu.

Why the need for a lockdown or any of the restrictions then?

Something wasn't adding up, although he definitely changed his tune later on, you have to wonder if he had a word being said in his ear.

I remember catching the Richie Allen radio show one day and he played a clip from Dermot Murnaghan on Sky News where he spoke to Irish United Nation's Special Rapporteur, Fionnuala Ni Aolàin who is also in a Human Right's Lawyer and she said that such was the speed that the legislation was prepared it was almost like it had been sitting in a drawer waiting to be used.

It appears others were also suspicious.

Whitty and his side-kicks Jonathan Van-Tam and Patrick soon became daily regulars on the T.V, giving updates on deaths, infections and cases.

Here's the trick though, are you ready? It's a good one.

They were counting every death within 28 days of a positive test as a Covid death.

Yes! Even if you were dying of Cancer, or dying of something else but tested positive with 28 days (basically a month) you went down as a Covid statistic.

Even if you showed no symptoms.

Now consider the number of people that you were told had died of this virus, and then consider what I have just told you.

What a disgrace.

See below:

CORONAVIRUS
Source: UK Government

49,044
total UK deaths
Deaths for any reason within 28 days of a positive test

They were inflating the numbers via the tests, the tests which were about as much use as a chocolate fire guard. They gave endless false positives that people would end up taking several times to identify clearly (or not) whether they had the virus or not.

When we eventually did have a phased return to some semblance of normality there was nothing stopping people using any liquid such as juice to get a positive test to enable them to get 10 days of work and paid for it.

I once did the test with Corona beer and funnily enough it came up positive.

What was to stop people who had gotten use to Furlough from doing this and continuing to inflate the numbers. The government most likely knew this would happen but as if they cared, it was furthering the scam.

If nobody tested, the scam wouldn't have had the foundations to build on and become anything like it was.

Some were absolutely obsessed with testing; it gave them some self-importance that they were **"doing their bit"**. It almost became a competition to see who could get Covid, I think they wanted others to feel sorry for them.

I remember once back at work that this guy I was working with said to me "I woke up at 1am last night with a sore stomach so I took a test but I'm fine".

I thought to myself "I wasn't aware needing a shit was a symptom", or maybe he was pregnant, who knows these days after all?

Conveniently the main test of choice was a PCR test which was invented by Kary Mullis.

Even he had this to say about them

"Anyone can test positive for practically anything with a PCR test, if you run it long enough... with PCR if you do it well, you can find almost anything in anybody...it doesn't tell you that you're sick."

Kary Mullis died on August 2019 of pneumonia aged 74.

Some might say that his death was convenient timing.

Dominic Cummings, Chief Advisor to Prime Minister Boris Johnson, was caught driving during the lockdown from Durham to Barnard Castle.

When he was caught, he gave the reason that he made the hour-long trip to test his eyesight.

He wanted to test his eyesight, driving a car, with his wife and son in it with him.

Is it not easier to look out the window at a sign in the distance or a number plate and see if you can read it?

Of course, it is, but it was another lie.

A quick search of what is around the area of Barnard Castle and up pops GSK (Glaxo Smith Kline).

Hmmm....I wonder what he could have been doing there.

Just another one of those pesky coincidences.

Boris Johnson allegedly tested positive several times and had to self-isolate.

The deadly symptoms? A high temperature and a persistent cough, yet amazingly was still able to get through his speeches on television without spluttering even once.

You only have to look at the PPE contracts to see that some were in the know, friends in high places you might say.

It was one big game show and the public were the unaware contestants.

Opening up…

As the government had dangled the carrot of freedom in front of a desperate public for probably as long as they could before disobedience crept in, the restrictions were beginning to ease based on infections and vaccination rates.

The vaccine was the carrot, get it and you can go out and play.

People were lining up to take the new experimental mRNA vaccines.

I just didn't understand it. Most people I knew were taking it go on holiday, but i felt they were completely missing the point. The thought they wouldn't get abroad without it so they injected something into their body that normally takes 7-10 years of development but was supposed to have been made in the space of a few months.

They were willing to take something that could potentially kill them or injure them for the rest of their lives just for the sake of some sea and sand.

I couldn't get my head around it.

If they waited and refused, the restrictions may have got tighter but this is where non-compliance comes in.

If we all said no, there is not a thing they could do

It's the many against the few and unfortunately, we have allowed the few to centralise their power for too long and do everything they say and jump at every say so.

It's time we remembered how to say no.

I'm not ignorant to the fact that people trust their governments and may not have looked into the things that I may have.

And to be honest, you should be able to trust them.

But this isn't an ideal world and unfortunately people take advantage of others.

It goes back to what I was saying at the start about conflicts and wars, the public never want them but we are dragged into them by a few psychopaths at the top.

We just have to learn to say no.

And no means NO.

Half of these politicians can't even identify a woman, yet we think they have the intellect and common sense to govern the country you live in.

It's laughable if not so serious.

My first day back at the Primary School I was working on and those who had turned up early had got out their vans to get the craic.

I was apprehensive and for good reason.

We were laughing and joking and making light of the situation when one guy said "oops, better keep our distance". He was serious.

The whole group stepped back from each other.

It's started already I thought.

As David Icke says "sheep have a sheep dog to keep them in line, us humans keep each other in line".

The boss and the Contracts Manager eventually turned up, explaining that we will have to adhere to new site rules i.e., hand sanitising, social distancing, now having to eat our lunch in our vans and so on.

We all had to sign on a safety document which is standard these days but he placed a box of pens in the centre of the circle where we stood.

The Contracts manager raised his voice and said "right, if everyone can get a pen out the box when it's your turn to sign on". There it was, all the guys taking a pen out the box one by one and none of them noticed.

I said "we are all taking the pens out the same box, it makes no difference" in an attempt to highlight the ridiculousness of the whole situation but one of them said "that's right! We could all be passing it to each other!"

Anywhere you went even in the middle of the street on streetlights there were signs to social distance, walk this way or that way. Directional arrows were sprayed on paths and stickers on floors of any building you were entering.

People blindly followed the infantile instructions and went where they were told without an argument.

Need something at the other end of the cereal aisle? They'd go all the around instead of opposing the direction of the arrow.

All of this was bad enough, but you could almost laugh at it.

The test of compliance wasn't over.

There was "new" scientific evidence that face masks worked and prevented the spread of the virus. Bearing in mind these were introduced with the worst of the "pandemic" over with.

Imagine a putting a chicken wire fence up in attempt to stop dust from getting out. That's effectively how good they were, even if you did believe the official narrative.

There were absolutely useless.

I remember when they were first brought in as part of the rules and walking into the local supermarket before work, straight in the door without one and went about my shopping until I walked around the corner and here was a worker who looked like he was about to raid the British Embassy with the SAS.

He was wearing a proper full-face gas mask.

I couldn't help internally pissing myself laughing but then as I have said previously, this was the psychological damage being done through this constant fear campaign that was being propagated.

On my way out and a co-worker of nine was headed towards me and before I could say a word, he said in his Geordie accent

"Where is your mask, Scott?".

I told him to shut up and kept walking.

I can see how some wouldn't like the confrontation and would do it for an easy life.

It did get exhausting at times but I'm not going to do something that makes zero sense to me just because someone told me to.

When I reached the car park there was a young couple who must've been about 20 years of age and had just got of their car and you could see they were nervous and I could hear them discussing whether they should wear a mask or not.

I interjected and said "it's fine, you don't have to wear one, I was just in there". They looked at me, smiled almost gratefully and said thank you and walked in.

Haha! Get in there! Day 1 and I'm causing disruption to the plan already I naively chuckled to myself.

Of course, I wasn't but it felt good!

Eventually the staff started to challenge you in places and some people used to wear the Sunflower badges which showed you were exempt from wearing a mask or had a disability.

I used to just say I was exempt and most of the time that was fine, others I'd just keep walking and most of the time they couldn't keep up with the legs of my 6ft frame.

Occasionally I'd email my local MP Drew Hendry to try and at least get him to think critically and look at things with a common-sense point of view.

What a waste of time.

I pointed out to him that the Flu had disappeared completely whilst Covid cases continue to rise, therefore how can masks actually work?

He response was "well, to me they do".

As Albert Einstein once said

"Two things are infinite: the universe and human stupidity; and I'm not sure about the universe."

How can the measures be possibly working to eradicate a Flu completely but allow another to apparently thrive?

I'll save you the time, it can't.

That's a fact by the way, the seasonal Flu actually disappeared for a period. Either that or it was rebranded Covid-19.

I am of this view personally.

What's also contradictory is all those lobbying for Climate Change action and Net Zero have absolutely nothing to say about the number of masks being dropped in the street or the volume of them now in our oceans.

Where were the hazard bins for the disbandment of these horrible things, if it was as deadly as made out? There was also no concern for the children wearing these in schools.

It's disgusting.

These young kids in school will absolutely be no doubt affected by having to learn whilst them and their teachers wore these face coverings. No wonder there were "Ghost Children" as mentioned earlier, would you want to go to school with all this? Secondary school was bad enough for me.

And that's the thing, a virus so deadly that you can wear a face covering, it didn't even have to be a particular grade of mask, you could walk in with a pair of pants over your head and it would have been considered suitable.

There were occasional videos clips of world leaders being caught in the act and taking their mask off as soon as they thought they were off camera. They knew they did nothing to stop the spread of a virus and knew the whole thing was one big lie.

My first venture into a pub since re-opening was also an experience.

You had to wear a mask when stood up and then you could take it off when sat down, follow the arrows and be seated where you were told with no standing at the bar.

This was cutting edge science of course, as my sarcasm overflows.

I would laugh as people didn't follow the arrows when they went to the toilet and you could see the bar manager tut and curse as he tried to speak to them quietly, as shouting and singing was another method of spreading the virus according to Nicola Sturgeon.

If only she would shut up once in a while.

She actually wanted to cut the bottoms of doors in Schools to aid ventilation. No, I'm being serious, just opening the thing never occurred to her.

And these people are running our country? Give me strength.

They couldn't run a bath.

Ultimately this is what we needed though, the whole silliness of it all to shine through to enable people to laugh at it and see it for what it actually was.

Silly, that's what it was.

None of the rules made any sense and most people deep down knew it. It was inevitable that compliance would slowly dwindle and fade away as people met to discuss what they had been living through for the past few months and more.

There might be light at the end of the tunnel yet.

Who, Why, How?

Of course, I was sat at home and most of the time I had nothing to do so I began to use my time to look more into what was going on, who was behind it and why it was happening and also how the perpetrators would try and reach their goal.

I had found out that The Johns Hopkins Centre for Health Security in partnership with the World Economic Forum and the Bill and Melinda Gates Foundation hosted Event 201, a high-level pandemic exercise on October 18, 2019, in New York. The exercise showed areas where public/private partnerships will be necessary during the response to a severe pandemic in order to diminish large-scale economic and the societal effects.

Diminish the large-scale economic and societal effects?

They were having a laugh.

This exercise was carried out just six weeks before the first case of Covid-19 appeared. A coincidence? I think not. It was almost like people were being assigned their roles and scripts to play the in "pandemic" that was to come.

All the members involved, The John Hopkins Centre for Health Security, The WEF (World Economic Forum) and The Bill and Melinda Gates Foundation we instrumental in pushing the whole narrative.

Bill Gates is such a lovely philanthropist really, such a kind man that looks out for us all. Or is he?

He has been investing in vaccines for years now and for a man that seems to be so concerned with our health he sure does like the profit that they bring.

Here is an excerpt from CNBC's website from an interview they conducted with the billionaire-

"We feel there's been over a 20-to-1 return," yielding $200 billion over those 20 or so years, Gates told CNBC's Becky Quick on "Squawk Box" from the World Economic Forum in Davos, Switzerland. "Helping young children live, get the right nutrition, contribute to their countries — that has a payback that goes beyond any typical financial return."

A 20-to-1 return and he expects us to believe he is in it for the health of children? Yeah okay Bill, nearly had me there...

Here is another section from the article-

"As a comparison, Gates echoed what he wrote in an essay in The Wall Street Journal last week under the banner "The Best Investment I've Ever Made," saying that same $10 billion put in would have grown only to $17 billion over 18 years, factoring in reinvested dividends."

I know what you're thinking, what's another 7 billion dollars right?

He then goes on to say this in the article-

"On vaccines, Gates also had a message for parents who fear side effects as a reason not to get their kids their shots. "It is wild that just because you get misinformation, thinking you're protecting your kid, you're actually putting your kid at risk, as well as all the other kids around them."

Is he more concerned about his investment or the children's health of whom he will be injecting?

There have even been pictures taken of Gates with the book How to Lie with Statistics by Darrell Huff in the foreground. He is trolling us, big time.

The tentacles of Bill Gates reach everywhere, including many media outlets. Why would he be interested in funding media? Let's face it, broadsheets like The Guardian were dying and everything is going online, with news being found on social media these days.

My argument is that you would only want to fund or back such outlets if you wanted to steer a narrative. He almost reminds me of the organisation, SPECTRE in the James Bond films, he is everywhere.

Go on any of Bill Gates' social media pages and you'll see that the comment section is turned off. He wouldn't want you knowing what others think of him as you might just catch onto what he is really up to.

He also attended number 10 Downing Street on multiple occasions and you have to wonder what influence he has over our government and its decisions.

He has no medical qualifications, yet is asked questions by the media as if he is some sort of Oracle, whilst many qualified professionals such as those who are involved with the Great Barrington Declaration are demonised or ignored.

James Corbett of The Corbett Report has made an outstanding documentary called Who Is Bill Gates? And I highly recommend everyone watches this to really understand the evil human being who guises himself as philanthropist and how he has monopolised global health.

His father Bill Gates Sr, served on the board of the Planned Parenthood Federation and interestingly in his book called *Showing Up for Life* he says:

"Every corner we've turned in the field of global health, we've found that the Rockefellers were already there and had been there for years.

When we committed to childhood immunization, we found ourselves building on efforts the Rockefeller Foundation had helped launch and fund in the 1980s.

When we became interested in fighting malaria and tuberculosis, we learned that the Rockefellers had been studying the prevention and treatment of such diseases around the globe for, in some cases, as long as a hundred years.

A similar dynamic held true in the case of HIV/AIDS.

A lesson we learned from studying and working with the Rockefellers is that to succeed in pursuing audacious goals you need like-minded partners with whom to collaborate.

And we learned that such goals are not prizes claimed by the short-winded. The Rockefellers stay with tough problems for generations."

There you have it, quite openly discussing working with the Rockefeller family to apparently fight diseases and save the world.

Why is it in 2023 where hygiene and medical knowledge has never been better, we seem to have more diseases, illnesses and new conditions than ever before?

I'm sure the Gates and Rockefeller families have a rough idea, as there is one thing Big Pharma doesn't want you to be, and that is fit and healthy.

The aforementioned Rockefellers have had their own almost prophetic exercises and documents regarding pandemics including the publication of Rockefeller Foundation Scenarios for Future Technology And

International Development which was exposed by investigative journalist Harry Vox, and discusses a world of tighter top-down government control and more authoritarian leadership with limited innovation and growing citizen pushback, with governments working in lock-step.

As you read through the document it plays out a scenario where a virus has come from an animal and spreads round the world, with it even mentioning China faring better than most due to its enforcement of mandatory quarantine for all citizens as well as near hermetic sealing off of its borders.

Have a look for yourself if you don't believe me:

It all sounds just a little too familiar doesn't it. Very familiar in fact and much like Event 201, it's almost like a

Scenario Narratives

LOCK STEP

A world of tighter top-down government control and more authoritarian leadership, with limited innovation and growing citizen pushback

In 2012, the pandemic that the world had been anticipating for years finally hit. Unlike 2009's H1N1, this new influenza strain — originating from wild geese — was extremely virulent and deadly. Even the most pandemic-prepared nations were quickly overwhelmed when the virus streaked around the world, infecting nearly 20 percent of the global population and killing 8 million in just seven months, the majority of them healthy young adults. The pandemic also had a deadly effect on economies: international mobility of both people and goods screeched to a halt, debilitating industries like tourism and breaking global supply chains. Even locally, normally bustling shops and office buildings sat empty for months, devoid of both employees and customers.

The pandemic blanketed the planet — though disproportionate numbers died in Africa, Southeast Asia, and Central America, where the virus spread like wildfire in the absence of official containment protocols. But even in developed countries, containment was a challenge. The United States's initial policy of "strongly discouraging" citizens from flying proved deadly in its leniency, accelerating the spread of the virus not just within the U.S. but across borders. However, a few countries did fare better — China in particular. The Chinese government's quick imposition and enforcement of mandatory quarantine for all citizens, as well as its instant and near-hermetic sealing off of all borders, saved millions of lives, stopping the spread of the virus far earlier than in other countries and enabling a swifter post-pandemic recovery.

script to which governments would follow and act accordingly.

Klaus Schwab, chairperson of the World Economic Forum and real-life Bond villain, with his bald head, suit and German accent. All that is missing is the spinning chair, white furry cat and a table with a big red button up in the Swiss Alps.

Schwab was born in Ravensburg, Germany in 1938 and is the Founder and Executive Chairman of the World Economic Forum which has events every year in Davos, Switzerland. It is where the rich and powerful gather to discuss the direction the world is headed, and such is the scale of the event that 5000 Swiss troops are used to ensure the security of the attendees.

Quite a paranoia given the good they claim to do for the world.

Schwab who describes George Soros of the Open Society Foundation as a mentor with the Hungarian-American having his own input at the Davos event by saying:

"Companies would "compromise themselves" in order to enter the Chinese market. That, he said, could lead to "an alliance between authoritarian states and these large, data-rich I.T. monopolies that would bring together nascent systems of corporate surveillance with an already developed system of state-sponsored surveillance. This may well result in a web of totalitarian control the likes of which not even Aldous Huxley or George Orwell could have imagined."

When you also find out Soros owns several thousand shares in Facebook, it's little wonder you couldn't voice your opinion about the pandemic response without being censored or banned from the social media platform. He has written multiple books on his and the World Economic Forum's vision for the world including Covid-19: The Great Reset where he discusses how the world will need to change to fight these new and increasingly occurring pandemics.

Schwab has famously said:

"The pandemic represents a rare but narrow window of opportunity to reflect, reimagine, and reset our world"

Even Prince Charles is pushing for The Great Reset:

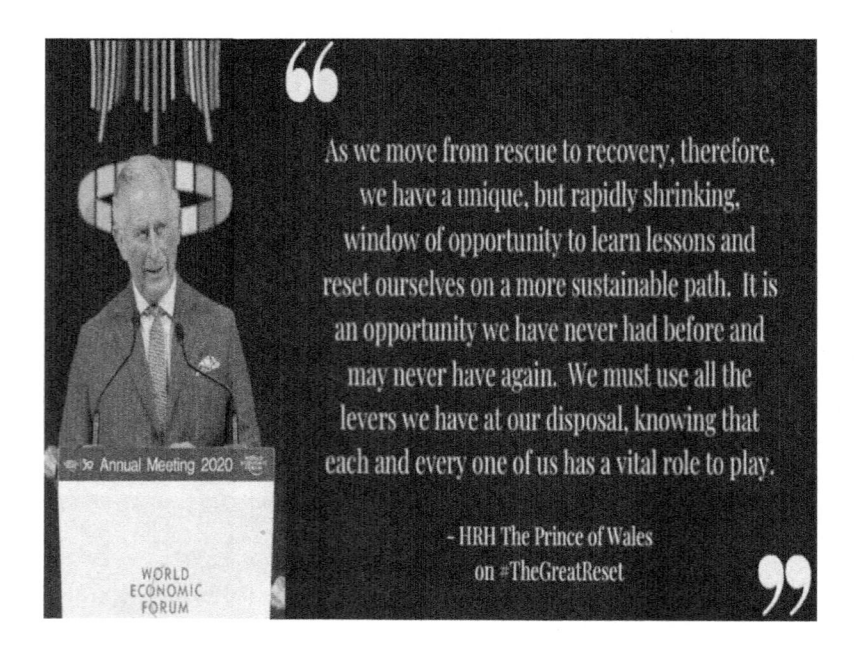

> As we move from rescue to recovery, therefore, we have a unique, but rapidly shrinking, window of opportunity to learn lessons and reset ourselves on a more sustainable path. It is an opportunity we have never had before and may never have again. We must use all the levers we have at our disposal, knowing that each and every one of us has a vital role to play.
>
> - HRH The Prince of Wales on #TheGreatReset

Note he says we have a unique, but rapidly shrinking, window of opportunity to basically reset the world. They know this is their chance, but if it drags on too long, they will have failed. They are racing for the finish line but in doing so they are also exposing themselves and their agenda greatly.

Yes, that was their plan along, problem, reaction, solution. The problem was allegedly a deadly virus, the reaction was to lock everyone down, and the solution was to vaccinate everyone, enforcing the constant update of vaccines via the passports which would then allow the next piece of the puzzle, which is CBDC or Central Banking Digital Currency.

I mean is it just another one of those coincidences that the British Chancellor who has plans for a CBDC called Britcoin is now the Prime Minister without even being elected?

Here is an excerpt from a Daily Mail article from the 24th July 2021:

"The Britcoin revolution! Rishi Sunak plans to introduce official digital currency to rival cash in 'biggest upheaval in the monetary system for centuries

Bank of England would establish a direct digital equivalent to physical money

Supporters say the move will give the economy a boost during a financial crisis

Could slash cost and time it takes to make payments online and transfer money

Cash in people's pockets would be superseded by a new 'Britcoin' digital currency in a plan being pushed by Chancellor Rishi Sunak.

Its supporters in the Treasury say that it would allow the Bank to give the economy a boost in times of financial crisis by paying the 'Britcoins' directly into people's bank accounts"

That sounds really nice of them, doesn't it? As I said before, they sell things by highlighting its convenience before the mission creep comes in, tightening the noose. You only have to go back to earlier in the book to see what I said about the whole control aspect of it.

The World Economic Forum isn't shy in declaring it's plans and visions for the world either, often displaying well-made videos on its social media telling us that insects are the future diet for us pesky peasants, 15-minute cities, social credit systems, and concrete jungles that we have to look forward to. Don't get too excited as you won't own any of it, oh no, there most famous video of all describes citizens "owning nothing and being happy", we will rent what we need in future.

It doesn't sound very happy to me.

You only have to listen Schwab's advisor Yuval Noah Harari for five minutes to realise the guy is a total psychopath.

Previously he has spoken of transhumanism (combining man and A.I) and the 4th industrial revolution or 4IR which the UK government has signed up to. He has also talked about a "useless class" (as he puts it) in economic terms and in my view that is exactly what they are aiming to achieve with Artificial Intelligence taking over many jobs through the said revolution.

Why is it that transhumanism is popping up more and more? Why do people like Elon Musk look to develop chips to put in people's brains in his Neuralink program?

We have already been sucked in by our Smart phones and we are already in the phase of the wearables and I'm sure you gather what the next phase will be.

You guessed it, implantable!

In Sweden some of the populations are already taking part in chipping parties. This is where the person gets a chip under the skin on the back of the hand and they can use to pay and all sorts of things.

It is my opinion that this is why Sweden was one of the few countries to not lockdown, as their population is already in the frame of mind of accepting technology into their bodies.

Harari has actually once said

"If governments succeed in hacking the human animal, the easiest people to manipulate will be those who believe in free will."

He also said this in a BBC interview:

"The coronavirus pandemic could prove to be a watershed event in terms of enabling greater surveillance of society.

People could look back in 100 years and identify the coronavirus epidemic as the moment when a new regime of surveillance took over, especially surveillance under the skin which I think is maybe the most important development of the 21st Century, is this ability to hack human beings."

Biometric data would create a system that knew human beings better than they knew themselves, he added.

READ THAT AGAIN and you will realise he is telling you exactly what their psychotic plan is. Once you understand the plan and see where it's going you also begin to see that many things are sold as a convenience then the belt soon tightens.

A prime example is the internet, a brilliant invention where we can communicate with loved ones all round the world and find an unimaginable amount of information, but look at the current push for the Online Safety Bill in the UK, they argue that it's to do with online bullying and trolls when it's anything but.

It's a tiptoe to digital I.D where governments can watch your every move and every single person in the world will need one to use the world wide web.

As I have said before you had got to hand it to them, it's almost perfect.

I can hear you saying how did they get all these politicians to carry out the plan? The World Economic Forum has a Young Leaders of Tomorrow program where many of the leaders you see around the world today have come through including Macron, Jacinda Ardern, Justin Trudeau, and even Vladimir Putin.

It is also my opinion that Jeffrey Epstein or similar types may have played a similar role in blackmailing politicians/figures in vulnerable positions, collecting the evidence whether it be pictures of videos and threatening to make them public should they not do as they are told.

Bill Gates has been to Epstein's Island multiple times and met with him on many occasions, even photographed with him, with Gates even admitting after him and his wife Melinda's recent split that she wasn't happy about their relationship, although Gates claims to have met Epstein for dinner to talk about business only.

Whatever you say Bill.

Digital I.D is the key to everything and without it, no cashless society can be implemented or the digital control system that they want to introduce without it.

This was the whole reason behind the attempt to get everyone vaccinated with the mRNA technology and bring in the vaccine passports in my opinion and Big Brother Watch did a great job of exposing the backdoor in them, effectively acting as a social credit system with different sections in within the digital passport including your criminal record. So much for health, eh?

Where Next?

Eventually there was some kick back and thankfully more and more were beginning to see this for exactly what it was.

A scam.

Protests began to happen all around the world with people sick to death of all these ridiculous rules and restrictions effectively putting a halt to people's lives.

Matt Hancock the former Health Secretary actually went on live T.V and pretended to cry such was his joy that vaccines were becoming available.

Does this man look genuine to you?

These bastards stole precious time of your lives that you will never get back, ever.

Remember this and never forget it.

Families have been divided, jobs lost, peoples mental health down the drain, economic destruction, people getting beaten in the street by Police and now getting killed because of these experimental injections with excess deaths currently running at 30% higher than normal.

On the 18th January 2023, the Telegraph published an article which said

"Deaths in England and Wales were 30 per cent higher than expected in the first week of January, with nearly 3,500 more registered than normal statistics show"

There is no daily death count for those people though, quite simply because it doesn't fit the narrative.

Many of these people were pressured into getting the jab by the way. Want to keep your job and put food on the table? Go get the jab or you're gone. Many people acted in such a disgusting manner and no doubt some people will be filled with regret and ashamed.

I believe though that most people are inherently good and the fact is most were just duped. It was the biggest psychological operation in history and I think sometimes it's easy to forget that. They literally threw everything at us in the last three years.

There are people I have known my whole life and they are the nicest people you could meet, but they just thought the government had their best interests at heart and believed what they were saying. Of course, now many of these people don't think that, and it has absolutely shattered their whole belief system. It's a shock to know everything you thought you knew is a lie and it affects everything you do, socially, politically, the company you keep, because all of a sudden, the inconsistencies I speak of are all of a sudden seen everywhere.

We need to guide these people who are slowly becoming aware of what's going on, not mock them.

It's the old cliché, divided we fall, united we stand.

Thankfully we had many people who were aware of what was going on and have had some amazing stories of courage and defiance rise to the surface above the barrage of propaganda.

The Canadian Truckers, the Dutch Farmers, the French standing up for their rights as the government attempts to raise the pension age without so much of a vote, and of course our own protests where many of us met others just looking for some solace knowing that they were not alone.

I remember leaving a protest once and I decided I was going for a pint after when I saw a woman who was there also who had just protested about masks yet was wearing one to get on the bus. I understand people don't want confrontation, but we have to say no. An unequivocal NO, with zero room for movement.

Give them an inch and they will take a mile. We have seen this; we know the drill and we must never allow it to happen again.

We will be in a perpetual crisis until they win, fail or we say no, enough is enough.

I believe the current Ukraine/Russia conflict is acting as a distraction from the damage being caused by the vaccines and also to further the agenda. Countries around the world have given Ukraine millions whilst their leader in Volodymyr Zelensky has rolled out the red carpet to anyone who will turn up in Kiev, whilst at the same time our very own Prince Charles cancelled his visit to Paris recently due to ongoing protests about the pension age.

It's a word I don't want to exhaust but it really is those inconsistencies again.

The UK is currently in a cost-of-living crisis but recently BAE boss scooped a £10.7m bonus with shares in UK's biggest defence firm soaring after Russia's invasion of Ukraine.

There is always money for war.

There are signs for encouragement though, leaders who were very authoritarian such as Nicola Sturgeon and Jacinda Ardern have resigned from there positions whilst Emmanuel Macron could be on his way and I'd say it's surely a matter of time before Justin Trudeau is gone from power too.

Early on it was discouraging, but with stories of heroes such as the Truckers and Farmers we now have to look one way and that is up.

Their race to the finish line with the prize for first being the global control of the population has triggered a mass awakening and once you can see beyond the lies there is no unseeing it.

We can see these people and their plans for what they are and they know more of us can see it daily so expect things to speed up.

Don't lose hope as we will get there, we just have to keep our spirits high and fight this with everything we've got.

My brother said to me at one point "that's it, we are done aren't we, finished, that's it".

I reminded him that at the start of the first hard lockdown, there were 5 of us who gathered and were surrounded by Police knowing something wasn't right.

We were ridiculed in the local papers.

But now there are millions of us.

We can do this.

REFERENCES

Images

https://twitter.com/Dawn51940357/status/1638849921976619009?t=N_mLR2sINPjQvvkr1YNeA&s=19

https://twitter.com/lisareality1/status/16389021629850378 26?t=GJYf0WzJyvw58Hgfua2oJw&s=19

https://twitter.com/lisareality1/status/16389021629850378 26?t=GJYf0WzJyvw58Hgfua2oJw&s=19

https://twitter.com/JamesMelville/status/1325724338134405120?t=ivymwYcom25Kwto3KVuOKQ&s=19

https://www.siasat.com/who-chief-highlights-collaboration-data-sharing-defeat-ncov-1820467/

https://metro.co.uk/2020/09/01/holly-willoughby-reunites-phillip-schofield-hugs-plastic-sheet-morning-13205646/?ito=article.mweb.share.top.link

https://www.manchestereveningnews.co.uk/news/greater-manchester-news/manchester-clap-heroes-nhs-coronavirus-18071785?utm_source=linkCopy&utm_medium=social&utm_campaign=sharebar

https://www.coventrytelegraph.net/news/health/mum-named-shamed-neighbours-missing-18144490?utm_source=linkCopy&utm_medium=social&utm_campaign=sharebar

https://www.bbc.co.uk/news/uk-52012432

https://twitter.com/imperialcollege/status/1056456818363453440?t=B77bQykAzXw74ersJy82kQ&s=19

https://eu.usatoday.com/in-depth/news/2020/04/08/through-window-world-shaped-coronavirus/2949871001/

Rockefeller scenarios for the future of technology and international development

https://www.gov.uk/government/speeches/pm-address-to-the-nation-on-coronavirus-23-march-2020

https://www.gov.uk/guidance/high-consequence-infectious-diseases-hcid

25-options-for-increasing-adherence-to-social-distancing-measures-22032020.pdf

https://www.cygnethealth.co.uk/news/impact-of-lockdown-on-childrens-mental-health-revealed/#:~:text=There%20an%20increase%20in%20the,was%20seen%20in%20disordered%20eating.

https://www.gov.uk/government/speeches/pm-statement-on-coronavirus-16-march-2020

https://www.kingsfund.org.uk/publications/nhs-hospital-bed-numbers

https://www.telegraph.co.uk/news/2023/01/18/deaths-england-wales-30-per-cent-higher-expected-first-week/

https://castbox.fm/x/2-THo (Richie Allen Show)

https://www.corbettreport.com/gates/ (Who is Bill Gates)

Printed in Great Britain
by Amazon